THE
LOVE
I LET GO

~MEHEK QURESHI

To everyone who's ever loved in silence,

Your story mattered even if it was never heard.

There are love that are loud, bold, fearless, and then there are the quiet one. This book is a collection of that quiet kind of love, that patient kind of love, the silent kind of love. This book is more of a grief, more of ache of letting go. The part that went missing after being detached to them, but the after-healing effect after not being compromising your love, your care on one who don't care. The love that grew in silence that never asked to be named, that bloomed quietly in the dark and wilted just the same. This book was born from that kind of love, from that kind of ignorance. These poems are not declarations. They are echoes. Echoes of moments that almost became something.

Dear Reader,

Thank you for picking up this book. I don't know your name, your story, or what led you to these pages, But I hope something here feels like home. This is not just a collection of poems. You might find pieces of your own silence here too. Those things you wanted to say but didn't, Or the beauty of loving someone with no expectations at all. If you've ever loved in silence, if you've ever walked away with your heart full but your lips closed

Then I want you to know this, you are not alone. You were never foolish. There is courage in quiet love. There is poetry in restraint. And there is healing in letting it live even if only on paper

Some people fall in love loudly. You see it in the way they smile, in the way they talk about that person constantly, in the way they hold hands in public and make it known: "I love them. "But not all of us are like that. Some of us fall in love quietly. We don't say it. We don't show it. We just feel it silently, deeply, entirely. I didn't even realize it at first. It started with small things: the way you looked when you were focused, the way your voice softened when you spoke kindly, how you made a room feel warmer without even trying. And suddenly, you were everywhere. In my thoughts. In the songs I heard. In the words I didn't say.

I didn't fall with noise. I fell with silence. And somehow, that silence was louder than anything I've ever known.

The thing about loving in silence is that it doesn't stop. It keeps growing even when it's not returned. Even when you know it can't be. There were moments I wanted to tell you. But how do you say "I love you" when you're not even sure if you're allowed to feel that way? So kept it inside.

I smiled when you smiled at someone else.

I listened when you talked about things that didn't include me.

I laughed with you, stood beside you, acted normal.

But inside, I was drowning in everything I couldn't say.

Some people scream their love into the world.

And some like me write books about it,

Because That's the only way we know how to speak.

Then, there comes a moment slow, cruel, and sharp when the truth sinks in, they will never be yours. Not the way you imagined. Not the way you dreamed in the quiet corners of your heart. And it doesn't happen all at once. It's not one big heartbreak.

It's a series of small cracks,

When they tell you about someone they like,

When they look through you instead of at you,

When they talk about a future, you're not in.

You smile. You nod. You pretend you're okay.

Because what else can you do?

You never told them.

They never promised you anything.

They never even knew.

But you know.

You know how deeply you loved.

You know what it cost you to carry all that feeling inside.

And now, you also know

That loving someone doesn't always mean you get to keep them.

"In a world full of faces, yours is the only one I see,

A radiant light that shines bright, illuminating me.

Everything else fades into darkness, a blurry haze,

 You are the dream that I've found, my heart's gaze.

Illusions of memories that never were
Echoes of a love that's not there

 Time ticks on, and I slowly fade

 A slow poison dissolving through my veins
Though I know we'll never be near

My heart loves deeply and holds you dear

In those honey brown eyes, a rainbow
shimmers divine,

 A refuge from loves endless roam,

 I find my home with every glance, my love
grows

 At last, I dare to steal, a last glance of it,

Last, but it seems infinite a ignite of fire
divine

The spark that beholds me, like an autumn
leaf

Hanging to the trees, but daring to fall
Unrequited,

yet my heart holds tight, A flame that
burns,

Through endless night Yet in your brown
eyes

I'll stay, forever lost, in their lovely sway

In the night shadows, I wait and hide
invisible to you,

like a ghost inside A secret admirer,

forever true Longing for moments that
never shines through

"Not everyone is meant to walk with us forever, and that's okay."

Your presence is vast and overwhelming, a
beauty to behold,

 A treasure to cherish, a love that never
grows old.

I was lost in the shadows, searching for a
glimpse of light,

 Until I found you, my guiding star, my
beacon in the night...

Falling for someone silently, and deeply is like knowingly

Gulping that poison down the throat,

Like those airport goodbyes, which we say and, hope that they would return back one day.

Like someone on death bed, who wants to live ,

Who wants to travel more around and know the world.

Like meeting your grandparents and not knowing which goodbye,

Could be the last Farwell.

The sea was silent

But the noise in my head was too loud,

My eyes were close but the picture of him
was as clear as a stream in my eyes.

My hair was floating in the air,

As if the essence of his aura was present
still in the air.

 I wasn't thinking about anything,

But his memories were prolonged in my
brain,

The fog was freezing but the eyes of him
were still staring at me.

I'm sitting under the roof while waiting for the sun,

While having moon standing at my window.

You were the one who used to colour the sky,

My love, as a colour blind how would I have known that u are going to change your colour.

There is feeling, made by misunderstanding

I'm here, you are also somewhere here

Habits doesn't change so quickly,

Feeling like my destiny was from journey to journey,

In my life you are the loss,

U were the house, now where should I knock?

I was the dark night meanwhile he the
dream of illusion in that night

An illusion born, fades in front of open eyes

I was lost in the sea of thought, Drowning in
the depths

His hand reaches, saves me tight, In
morning dreams, a gentle might.

In the darkness of mine, he shines,

A constellation or the sheet of illusion
around which I used to cover myself.

In starry nights, I search for signs,

A message from your heart's aligned.

But like constellations, we're apart,

A celestial distance, in my heart.

Wanting to move on, yet stuck in time,

Trapped in love's labyrinth, no escape to
find.

Torn between dreams and harsh reality,

Incomplete stars, my painful symmetry.

Your eyes, like sapphire shines so bright
 My guiding light, through endless night.
Though unrequited, love remains,
 Forever yours, in silent refrains.

From my perspective, this love's divine,
A bittersweet symphony, intertwined.
Yours, unknowingly, my heart's rhyme,
Forever entwined, in this starry crime.

It was your eyes, too. Not just the way they looked at me, but the way they truly saw me. There was something in them a softness, a knowing that made me feel like I was something fragile and rare, like I was worth protecting even on the days I didn't believe it myself. In your gaze, I felt seen, not just noticed. Safe, not just admired.

Now, I see those eyes only in dreams, like distant memories trapped in faded photographs. They're still beautiful, still shining in my mind, like stars that burn bright long after they've died out. But that's the hardest part they're no longer mine. They belong to a past I can't touch anymore, only remember

"Some eyes don't just see you. they save
you.

And losing them feels like losing home."

When we fall in love with stranger, a
stranger,

But completely known to our heart, known
to our eyes.

We engrave their name deep into our heart,
deep into our veins,

But when it slowly grows, it becomes
madness,

Madness which led to death, which tares
our soul apart.

The words that you spoke are still alive in
my poems,

I try not to read those poems, but once at
some point,

I always find myself between those pages.

Loving someone and dedicating a song to them is the most heart wrenching you can do because every time when you listen that song, you not just hump that song,

You constantly, knowingly or unknowingly remember them.

It's like you start visiting those moments which had become memories

A graveyard of memories, a cold hug to our heart.

You loved them as, that series or movie
which you re-watch

You keep re-watching it even if you know
the ending,

You know how things going to end, then
also you keep making yourself delusional.

"They said to let go

Is the best you can do "

But is it that easy? I ask you is that really that easy, loving someone deeply

By our soul deep into our heart whose names runs like blood in our veins.

And then one day we ask ourselves our soul to let go off them, to set them free

But letting go is not the same for everyone, one who can leave everything

And set their self-free in one sec, while one to whom it's been years since they visited that Place without thinking of them, to watch a movie and not remember their laugh,

Some takes a moment to forget, while some takes years and still struggles

With it. That's okay but that's completely okay what not is making yourself suffer

By visiting those graves again and again which just keep killing you.

I loved you in the quietest way

So softly,

That world never noticed,

And neither did you.

Every "I'm happy for you "

was a lie I folded into smiles,

While watching you Choose

Everything

But me.

You spoke of people,

You spoke of heartbreaks,

You spoke of people who never saw you,

And I listened

Like someone who did

Because I did,

God knows I did.

I memorized the shape of your joy,

From a distance,

Clapped for your victories,

With bleeding hands.

I had whispered your name into my pillow

Which never whispered back.

You I'll never know,

How many times

I almost told you

How many times

I didn't

And maybe that's love too,

Not asking for anything,

Not demanding to be seen.

Just loving quietly,

 Even when it hurts,

Even it breaks you

Even, when they

Never knew.

"We meet people as strangers and sometimes carry them as memories for a lifetime."

There are moments when the world slows down just you, your coffee, and the pages of a familiar book. The words don't just tell a story; they echo the silences of your own heart. And somewhere between the lines, you remember them.

That one person whose love still lingers like the aftertaste of strong coffee, bittersweet, unforgettable. The one you once spoke about endlessly, the one who knew your laugh and your silence. They may be gone, but somehow, they live on in every sentence that makes your chest ache and your eyes water without warning.

You sip slowly, not just to savour the coffee, but to hold on to that memory for just a little longer.

I didn't know the last time,

Was the last,

Not when you laughed

Not when I touched your name,

Like a prayer I believed in.

I held on like sea hold for shore,

Carving myself,

Into someone,

You'll stay for.

I loved wrenching my heart,

Bleeding through my pillows,

But I forgot that,

Love is not kept,

By bleeding quietly.

Letting go isn't about pretending it didn't matter. It's not about deleting photos, erasing messages, or convincing ourselves we were never affected. Because we were. Deeply. What we had meant something, even if it ended, even if it broke us, even if it wasn't meant to last forever. Letting go is not about denying the impact it's about learning to live with it in a way that doesn't hurt every time we remember.

It's about learning to carry the memory without letting it carry us. About allowing ourselves to feel the ache without letting it control our every thought. We begin to understand that healing doesn't demand forgetting, it demands understanding. We start to see that memories can live in us like soft echoes still there, still present, but no longer loud enough to drown out the sound of our own heartbeat.

Letting go is not brave,

It's Not poetic,

Its staring at a door

That won't open again,

 Choosing one breath at a time

And not to knock.

I begged the silence,

For answer you never gave,

Measured my worth,

In every glance you didn't send back,

every "maybe" I turned into "more"

World is vain for me, I'm still sitting at the sunset

While being upset from sun

You were the gift of my patience,

 It was always for you, by you

If now you hide something, how would I know dear?

"Loving someone who can never be yours
is like standing at the edge of the shore,
day after day, eyes fixed on the horizon. You
wait for a ship that has long sailed away a
ship that was never meant to dock for you.
The waves crash and retreat, echoing your
silent hope, but they bring no message, no
sign. The one you wait for doesn't even
know you're there. They've never looked
back. And yet, you stand heart heavy, soul
anchored in a dream that only you carry.
Because sometimes, love isn't about being
seen. It's about feeling so deeply, even in
the shadows."

This innocent heart need rest sometimes,

Maybe that this time he comes he doesn't
leave wrenching it

It roams around, but still only beats for you,

Don't stop it, let it get hurt

It will be roaming again, and again

There is everything, everyone, but the only
regret,

That eats me alive, is the grief of your
absence.

There are many sins in my faith, but the joy of having you was compensation of it

Now should I repent over it, or "should I be gone again to the same way?"

This heart always felt,

There is everything, but the emptiness of
you not being present make them nothing

There is everything, but the repentance, the
grief of not having you destroys their worth.

There is a room, filled with emptiness,

With the illusion, dream of you being with
me.

A room in my house is empty, waiting for
you.

Waiting in the will, that one day you knock
on it.

Life is the name of repentance, grief, which
lives in the poem mentioning you

All my poems are named on you, on the
zenith of grief of our loved

Liquor is just the excuse of addiction,

 the real addiction the real loss is to see
you walk away.

As we move forward, trying to rebuild ourselves and reshape our lives, there's often a quiet resistance from within. It's not always loud or dramatic. sometimes it's just a memory, a scent, a song, or an old photograph that pulls us back. Even when we're doing our best to grow and evolve, some invisible thread keeps tugging at us, drawing us toward the past. Toward the comfort we once knew. Toward them.

It's not that we don't want to let go. In fact, many of us try hard to do exactly that. We fill our days with distractions, chase new goals, and surround ourselves with people. But deep down, a part of us still aches for what was. We remember the way their presence filled a silence, how their voice softened the rough edges of a bad day, how we felt seen even if only for a moment. That longing doesn't disappear just because time has passed. In some cases, time only makes it heavier.

There was someone who wasn't home
yesterday.

And then here is me, Living in illusions,

Conversing with memories,

Hoping the shadows might turn into you.

This heart

It doesn't rest anymore.

It trembles at the sound of your name,

As if it remembers the way you once held it

I accept all loneliness, all repentance, as a faith

But still will be waiting for hours at the shore,

 so that one day you come and take me with you

All these causes only this innocent heart,

which smells like the graveyard of regret,

Neither he reads those poems, nor he understands the feeling.

There are letters hidden in my drawer,

Each word soaked in quiet sorrow,

Each page bleeding with the ache

Of being unknown by you.

Should I set them on fire,

Let their ashes rise to the sky like a prayer?

Or will the grief within those letters,

Crawl into my lungs,

And burn me alive from the inside out?

You told me your story,

Every wound, every fall, every scar.

But the silence of my pain

Still echoes in the hollow chambers of my soul.

You moved on,

And I stayed behind,

Stuck in a place where your name,

Is both my sanctuary and my storm.

way you let it go, they say there's a cure for everything.

A remedy for pain.

A fix for wounds.

But for me

There's only you.

There is everything around me.

Life continues, The world spins,

The sun rises. But in your absence,

Everything turns hollow.

Things exist, but their meaning has vanished.

And in their place remains

Only repentance,

And the unbearable grief

Of not having you.

The past has a strange power. It wraps itself around us in ways we don't always recognize until we try to leave it behind. And when we finally do, when we take even one brave step forward, it follows us like a shadow. Not to haunt us, but to remind us that healing isn't linear. That progress doesn't mean forgetting. And that sometimes, the reason we feel so lonely now isn't because we're alone, but because we remember what it felt like not to be.

The past may knock, but I don't break,

Not every scar becomes an ache.

Some wounds have taught me how to breathe,

How to stay soft, and still not bleed.

They speak of a love, that was never truly known,

Of a voice, that was never truly heard.

Should I burn all those poems?

Watch them curl into ash,

Let the flames swallow

What I was never brave enough to say?

Or will their grief rise instead,

Turn into smoke

And live in my lungs

Until I suffocate on silence?

You spoke your truth, Poured it like rain

On a garden I couldn't reach. But my pain?

My story?

It sat quietly at the edge,

Unseen,

Unspoken.

Still bleeding beneath my smile.

This heart, it doesn't beat the same.

It shivers, Like a cold wind through a
broken window

Yes, I have everything, A life,

A laugh, A hundred distractions.

But without you, everything feels like
nothing.

I carry the one thing I can't let go

Regret.

The kind that festers.

The kind that rewrites every "what if"

Until it becomes a curse.

Because the worst kind of loneliness

Isn't being alone,

It's being forgotten

By the one "soul."

You can't forget.

There is a love that never finds a voice. A love that lives entirely in the quiet corners of our hearts, for someone who doesn't even know we exist. It may sound strange to others, even foolish. How can you love someone who has never looked into your eyes? Never heard your voice? But it happens. More often than we admit.

It starts with admiration. A smile, a kindness, a way of being. We begin to imagine them in our world, not because they promised us anything, but because their presence sparked something we didn't know we were missing. We love silently, from a distance, building a version of them in our minds. One that fits the spaces in us that long to be filled.

This kind of love is tender but also painful. There's no place to put it. No text to send. No confession to make. Just a feeling that keeps growing, with nowhere to go.

It teaches us something too that love isn't always about being chosen back. Sometimes, it's about discovering the capacity of your heart to feel deeply, without expectation. To care, even when it's quiet. And to understand that even the most silent love still says something about who you are someone capable of seeing beauty where others may not look.

I'm still learning who I am. Not the version people want me to be, not the mask I wear to make others comfortable but the real me. The one who feels deeply, dreams recklessly, and fears being misunderstood. It's a slow process, peeling away the layers of approval and expectation. But in the quiet moments, I catch glimpses of him and he's worth fighting for.

It creeps in silence, not with sound,

But in the places, I thought I'd drowned.

Old streets, old songs, old shades of light,

Pull me gently into night.

The scent of rain on thirsty stone,

The kind we shared when we were alone.

A voice that sounds like yours, but not,

Still, my heart forgets what time forgot.

I buried you in folded clothes,

In books unread, in poems closed.

But memory has a cruel kind hand,

It lets me breathe, then makes demands.

I wrote you in glances, in moments you
never saw.

In the way my eyes searched for you,

Though yours never paused.

You were a page I dared not turn,

A song I only hummed.

A sunrise I admired quietly,

Afraid to name what it had become.

No petals plucked, no vows made,

Just a soft ache, and a smile that stayed.

Love, not in presence, but in the idea—

Of someone who never knew they were
home.

Sometimes we love quietly, not because we're weak, but because we respect the space between us and them.

Because we know that not all love is meant to be claimed, some is meant to be cherished, like a favourite song that no one else understands.

Loving someone who doesn't know you can feel lonely, but it also reveals the depth of your own heart. It shows that you're capable of care, beauty, and hope, without ever asking for anything in return, and maybe, that's the most honest kind of love there is.

People say loving someone silently, is easy

But here's what no one tells you, that kind of love takes strength. Real strength.

To love without being loved back.

To feel deeply without expecting anything in return.

To see someone's beauty and never ask them to notice you.

It may feel invisible, but it's not
meaningless. That silent love reveals
something powerful about who you are. It
shows that you are capable of seeing
magic in ordinary moments. That your
heart is wide enough to hold joy and ache
at the same time. That you don't love just to
be chosen you love because that's who you
are.

And maybe, just maybe, that silent love
was never wasted.

Because it shaped you.

It softened you.

It taught you how much tenderness your
heart is capable of.

So, if you've ever loved someone from afar, without ever telling them, without ever being seen don't call it foolish. Call it brave.

Because you loved.

And that alone makes you extraordinary.

I loved you like the quiet rain, falling soft
where no one sees.

A name I whispered in my mind, Like prayer
between the trees.

You never turned to look my way, No
glance, no word, no trace.

But still I watched you pass me by,

A universe in grace.

You didn't know I memorized, The rhythm
of your day

The books you held, the way you laughed,
the things you'd never say.

No petals dropped, no promises, no stories
ever spun.

Just feelings blooming silently, for
someone touched by none.

I wasn't in your orbit, love

Not even in your sky. But still I gave you all I
had,

Without the need for why.

And though you never knew my name, this
love still made me feel

That I could care so deeply for,

A dream that wasn't real.

Moving forward doesn't mean shutting the door on the past. It means walking forward with grace, carrying what shaped us without letting it weigh us down. It's honouring the love, the lessons, the versions of ourselves that existed in that time. And most importantly, it's learning how to grow from the cracks instead of being defined by them.

Because loneliness isn't always about being physically alone. Often, it's about who's missing from the story we once believed would last. It's about the gap between the life we imagined and the one we're left holding. It's about the conversations we still play out in our minds, the endings we never got to rewrite, the promises that never made it too forever.

And in that quiet space in that realization, we begin to see that loneliness has layers. It is complex and deeply human.

But it's also survivable. And with time, with gentleness, we begin to fill those empty

spaces with new hope, new people, and most importantly, a stronger version of ourselves

When I swam too deep into the ocean, taking my feelings for granted,

The waves should have pushed me out.

But no, I kept swimming deep, deeper

But when I tried to swim back to the shore,

I realized how far I had gone.

How far you did let me go alone.

And in that moment, I realized it was just me.

Me, lonely.

While you left me drowning in that deep ocean,

Searching for a new shore.

You had already left.

Left me drowning in that deep ocean,

While you searched for a brand-new shore.

A new thrill.

A new "me."

Maybe I was the droplet

That fell

Without ever touching your skin.

Without ever being noticed.

I thought you were the moment.

I swore you were the moment.

Until you turned into a memory.

I thought you were with me,

Until you vanished....

Like sand,

Slipping through the cracks,

Right in front of my eyes.

Love, I've learned, isn't fireworks or chaos. It's safety. It's sitting next to someone in complete silence and still feeling full. It's being seen in your worst moments and not flinching. It's a hand reaching out when you least expect it, eyes that say "I'm here" without a word. The world teaches us to chase intensity, but the real kind of love is soft steady the kind you can trust to stay.

Maybe I was the "flower you forgot to pluck."

Just another bloom.

Too ordinary for your bouquet.

Letting go isn't about pretending it didn't matter. It's about learning to carry the memory without letting it carry us. It's about moving forward while still honouring what shaped us. And in that balance, we begin to understand that loneliness, too, has layers. It's not always about who's around us now but who's missing from the story we once believed would never end with teary eyes,

I was picking up the pebbles of illusion,

One by one, Thrown by my mind,

So, they wouldn't shatter the glass of my dreams.

I built castles, out of everything you never said,

Held on to hopes,

You never meant to keep.

I painted your silence with colours I created, So I wouldn't have to face

The grey truth.

You,

You were never really mine, just a visitor in
my heart,

Leaving footprints,

Where I planted forever.

I kept watering empty promises,

Hoping they'd bloom into something real,

But even the rain,

Felt like it was crying for me.

Sometimes barely noticeable a familiar perfume in the air, the scent of something they used to wear, passing by us like a ghost. And suddenly, we're not in the present anymore. We're back in a memory, standing beside them, laughing, hurting, loving. Even if we were doing fine just a moment ago, that one breath of nostalgia can undo weeks of strength.

Perfume has that kind of power. It doesn't just linger on fabric it lingers on memories. It clings to nights spent talking under the stars, to hugs we never wanted to end, to the last time we saw them walk away. A scent can collapse time, bring back a version of us that no longer exists, and make us ache for someone we no longer speak to. We don't always realize how deeply a smell can root itself in our soul until it returns to us, uninvited and unforgettable.

And now,

Now I'm here,

Sitting at the edge of what we never were,

Learning how to swim,

Out of the ocean,

You left me in.

"For once try to find me into those dark night,

Maybe I'm still standing there for you."

Healing isn't loud. It's not dramatic or beautiful like people say. It's quiet, often lonely the kind of growth that happens when no one is watching. It's crying yourself to sleep and still getting up the next morning. It's learning to forgive yourself for the things you didn't know, and choosing over and over again not to let the past define you. Sometimes healing is simply choosing to keep going, even when your heart still feels broken.

Not everyone is granted the presence of their beloved.

Some are left with the chill of lonely nights,

With prayers resting on wet lashes, prayers that are never answered.

The echo of broken promises screams through the silence,

An ocean of desires that never reaches shore,

And a carnival of memories where every face becomes a wound.

Those for whom we once wished for the whole world,

In the end, become just an unfinished story,

One that's never complete, and never forgotten.

Some are left with a blanket of loneliness,

Stories written in the ink of sighs,

A river of tears,

An ocean of unfulfilled desires,

And a carnival of memories.

They become just a name etched on the
pages of time,

You were a chapter, not the end,

Yet every start feels like pretend.

The past outlives the present's claim,

And whispers softly in my name.

I smile, I speak, I carry on,

But some of me is always gone.

Left behind in ghost-filled rooms,

In yesterday's familiar gloom.

So here I am, both whole and torn,

A heart rebuilt, yet still worn.

Nostalgia isn't sweet or kind,

It's the shadow I can't leave behind.

Not everyone is blessed with the warmth of their beloved's hand in theirs.

Some are left walking through life with shadows as their only companions.

Shadows of moments that once held promise,

Now just flickering ghosts of what could have been.

There are those whose fate isn't written in shared laughter or eternal togetherness,

But in silent goodbyes, unsent messages,

And the echo of a name they no longer have the right to call out loud.

For them, love isn't a chapter with a happy ending,

But a storm that never passed, a wound that never closed,

A fire that keeps burning long after the other has walked away.

They don't sleep beside the one they love,

They lie awake haunted by memories that replay like lullabies sung by heartbreak.

Their dreams aren't of a future together,

But of alternate realities where things didn't fall apart,

Where timing was kind, and love didn't come with conditions.

For some, all they're left with is an ocean of unspoken desires,

A river of tears that no one sees,

And a marketplace of memories where every corner reminds them of what they lost.

They carry the weight of "almost,"

The sting of words left unsaid,

And the ache of loving someone who was never truly theirs.

And perhaps the most painful part?

They still love.

Deeply.

Silently.

Endlessly.

Even when the world has moved on,

Even when the one they love has forgotten them,

They hold on.

Sometimes,

The heart doesn't know how to let go of the only thing,

It ever beat for.

We move through the world trying to be strong, trying to stay present. We tell ourselves we've moved on, that we've let go. And maybe, most days, we have. But healing doesn't mean erasing the past it means learning how to live with it. It means recognizing that certain memories, like certain scents, will always stay with us. They will visit us in passing, sometimes gently, sometimes painfully. And that's okay.

Because loneliness, in its deepest form, often has nothing to do with the people around us. It comes from missing something so specific like the way they smelled when they hugged us goodbye, the way their perfume lingered in the room even after they left. It's not just about missing them. It's about missing the way life felt with them in it.

And yet, despite the weight I bear,

There's something softer in the air.

A gentler voice within my chest

That whispers: maybe this is rest.

Not all that fades is meant to die,

Some things leave so we can try.

To grow beyond what once confined,

To find what we were meant to find.

The movies. Not just the films, but what they meant. They were our quiet rituals, our escape, our language. You knew every line before it was said, laughed at the jokes as if you had lived them, cried at the parts that others overlooked. Watching a movie with you felt like being wrapped in something warm and safe, like time paused for us. But now, those same scenes feel foreign.

They're still playing, still ending the way they always did, but you're not beside me, mouthing the words or reaching for my hand. I can't press play anymore, because every frame reminds me of a chapter we never got to finish. The truth is those movies had endings, beautifully written and neatly tied up. But we... we just stopped. And there's no credits, no fade to black, no soundtrack to explain the silence you left behind.

"The movies ended, but we never got our final scene."

The echoes no longer demand my stay,

They rise, then slowly drift away.

I let them come. I let them go.

This time, I do not follow.

Because even in this shattered frame,

There's beauty blooming from the pain.

And though I miss what couldn't last,

I'm learning not to live in past.

So here I am, still not complete,

But standing steady on my feet.

With memory behind, and hope ahead,

And dreams to stitch the tears I've shed.

Sometimes, not getting love from the house we called home also built a lover who tries to put their love, their interest in everything and everyone but they forget that not every time the love we pour into a plant will give us same number of flowers. We never know that the flowers which we are growing is going to be a decor in someone's hair or would be garland on someone's grave.

My whole world revolves around you every thought, every heartbeat, quietly pulled in by your gravity. I move through life shadowing your light, loving you in silence, existing in the spaces you never look at. And still, I wonder... in all the vastness of your world, will you ever pause, even for a moment, and realize that I was there? That I existed, completely, for you?

There are days I feel like I'm made of glass standing in a room full of people, completely visible, yet never truly seen. I laugh, I nod, I speak when spoken to, but inside it's all echoes. I wonder if anyone ever really hears me, or if they're just listening to the version of me, they've made up in their heads. It's strange, how you can be surrounded and still feel like you're fading.

Love softened by truth and purified by pain
is a love that frees you. It frees you from
resentment, from bitterness, and from
endless questions with no answers. It frees
you from the need to hold on to someone
who is no longer meant to be part of your
path. When you step back without hatred,
you reclaim your power. You honour the
love you gave and the person you are
becoming.

You'll never know how deep this goes.

You'll never feel the weight I carry.

Of loving you in silence,

Of aching quietly

While you smile, unaware.

You'll wonder, "How could someone love
this much?"

But love like mine isn't measured,

It's endured.

It lives in every breath I take without you.

It breaks me every time you look away.

It rebuilds me when you say my name

Like it still matters.

I don't want the world.

I just want to matter to you.

But if love means losing,

Then let me lose myself completely,

Because even in pain,

Loving you is the only thing that feels like home.

You were the light I chased in dreams,

A distant star so far,

I reached with trembling, open hands,

But you never felt my scars.

I built a world of "what ifs,"

Where maybe you'd see me too,

But hope is fragile, slipping fast,

When loves not meant for two.

So here I stand, alone but wise,

Learning to let you be,

Unrequited love still burns,

But it won't destroy me.

Only those who've been insane in love truly understand what it means to give your heart away, even when it's breaking. I was one of them mad for you in a way that defied reason. I loved you like the moon loves the tide, pulling you close even as you drifted farther with every passing day. I knew the fire would never be mine, but I still flew into it like a moth, willingly, because some love is worth the pain it brings.

You may never know how often I whispered your name into the silence, how I folded you into every moment like a soft ache that never left. I didn't ask for forever I just wanted to matter to you, to be a pause in your chaos, a place your heart could rest. But love, no matter how pure, can't survive where it's not held back with equal hands.

There comes a time in every heart's journey
when holding on hurts more than letting go.
It's not because the love was false or
meaningless quite the opposite. It means
that love was real enough to teach you, to
break you, and to make you whole again.
But when the love you give isn't met in the
same measure, it's time to stop pouring
your heart into an empty well.

Letting go is not about giving up on love. It's
about giving yourself the chance to love
yourself fully. This isn't about anger, and
it's no longer about sadness. It's about
clarity and courage. It's about transforming
pain into wisdom and finding peace in the
truth that love, when it's meant to be, will
stay and when it's not, it must be released.

Remember, you were once the flame, burning bright and fiercely. You may have become the ashes when love ended. But now, you become the wind. The wind that rises, that carries the past away, and that brings new beginnings

"Letting go with love is not weakness." It's the deepest form of strength and it's how you begin again.

I whispered love in silent nights,

Hoping you would hear my heart,

But you never turned my way

I stayed alone, torn apart.

I watched you smile at someone else,

While I hid behind my fear,

Wishing I could be the one

Whose name you'd always hear.

Unseen, unheard, I loved you still,

A story left untold

A quiet ache that lingers on,

A heart that won't let go.

"I let go not because I stopped loving, but because I learned that love sometimes means walking away alone."

Life doesn't pause for aching hearts,

Nor wait for souls torn clean apart.

It marches on through storm and flame,

Unmoved by sorrow, loss, or shame.

You stood, they left and silence grew,

A hollow space once filled with "you."

But stars still blink, and winds still race,

And morning sun still warms your face.

The world keeps spinning, unaware

Of dreams once whispered in the air.

Yet in that spin, there's something true,

A hidden path ahead of you.

So let them go who couldn't stay,

Their story took another way.

Yours isn't done your fire remains,

Still burning through the deepest pain.

You're not behind, you're simply new,

A soul reborn, a clearer view.

The point of life is not to chase,

But find your peace, your time, your place.

Being alone is not the end,

It's not a sentence carved in stone.

It's where you meet the version of you

Who thrives in darkness all alone.

I held the world in trembling hands,

And dropped it with a single choice.

One moment changed the shape of time,

And silenced every hopeful voice.

I wish that I could turn it back,

Undo the bruise, erase the mark.

But fate is cruel with open wounds,

It leaves you walking through the dark.

They don't see the nights I cry,

The ache of guilt I've grown to wear.

They only see the broken thing,

Not the soul beneath repair.

But must I carry all this shame?

Must every sunrise punish me?

Can't mistakes just be the steps

We take toward who we're meant to be
with.

I am not perfect, I am pain,

But I am also breath and fight.

I stumble, bleed, and fall apart,

But still, I crawl back toward the light.

If life has taught me anything,

It's that forgiveness takes its time.

And though I made a thousand wrongs,

My heart still seeks a higher clam.

You looked at them with oceans wide,

With hopes that lit your every glance.

They looked away and found their peace,

In someone else's second dance.

You gave them poems made of stars,

A heart that beat with just their name.

But still, they left, and now you ask,

Was I too soft? Was I to blame?

You watched them fall for someone new,

Watched promises dissolve like rain.

You stood there smiling through the tears,

While hiding mountains made of pain.

It cuts so deep to not be picked,

To be the option left behind.

To give your all and still not be,

The one they say they want to find.

But hear me now, and hear it clear,

Their choice does not define your soul.

You are not lesser, not unseen,

Not broken, lacking, or not whole.

They couldn't see the fire you are,

The love you carry in your bones.

But someone else will see it all,

And know they've finally found their home.

So, grieve them, yes, but do not stop.

Your life's not written by their hand.

You are a story yet to bloom,

A love too vast to understand.

I don't light two cups of coffee anymore.

 The silence across the table is used to me.

But some mornings, I still reach,

As if your hand might be where it used to
be.

I don't check my phone like I used to,

Waiting for your name to bloom on the
screen.

But there are nights I still dream you back,

And wake up with your ghost in between.

You don't exist in this world anymore,

No number, no address, no flesh I can
touch.

But God, your memory still wears my shirts,

Still knows my heart like it's too much.

I see you in strangers, how they laugh,

In songs you hated, in rain-soaked days.

I see you in the places we never went,

In all the words I forgot to say.

Sometimes, I still talk to you. Not because I've lost my mind, but because love like yours doesn't leave quietly. I speak to you in the pauses of my day, in the middle of a song, when I see your favourite street dog, or when the sky turns the same colour, it did the last evening we laughed. I turn to share something with you, and then I remember you're not here. And somehow, that ache has become a part of me now.

I remember the way you loved me. Not in sweet poems or movie lines, but in the messy, breaking, beautiful way that only someone who really sees you can love. I was chaos loud, wounded, guarded and you were stillness. Not because you had no pain of your own, but because you made space for mine. I pushed you away more times than I can count, and every time, you stayed. Not to save me, but to remind me I was worth staying for.

You waited like time had no clock. You listened like silence was your first language. You held me not as someone broken, but as someone sacred. Even my ruins, even the parts I hated, you touched with kindness. And that kind of love it leaves a mark nothing else can match.

And now... I live. I wake up. I go through the motions. I laugh sometimes. But your absence walks beside me like a shadow. Loud. Unamicable. Every step I take, it's like you're echoing somewhere behind me. You don't exist anymore at least not in a way I can call or touch. But you're not really gone, either. You're woven into me now in the choices I make, the people I trust, the words I write when it gets too quiet.

You left me with fingerprints and flame with a love that still burns under everything. And I'll carry you. In love. In grief. In hope. Until the day I meet you again... or until the world makes me forget your name.

But I won't. I never could.

You're gone,

But you never really left.

You live in the pauses,

In the songs I skip,

In the places I avoid

Because they still smell like you.

You don't exist in this world anymore,

But in mine,

You echo.

And no matter how far time pulls me,

I'll carry you

In silence,

In memory,

In love

Love can be one of the most beautiful experiences in life but it can also hurt in ways we never expected. Maybe you gave your heart fully, only to feel abandoned. Maybe you loved deeply, only to be misunderstood. Maybe you're carrying memories that ache like fresh wounds, even though the people in them have long since gone.

If you're healing from love, know this: it's okay to grieve what could have been. It's okay to miss someone and still know they weren't meant for you. It's okay to feel broken even when you try to stay strong. Healing doesn't follow a straight line

it's slow, it's quiet, and sometimes it's messy. But that doesn't make it any less real or important.

One of the hardest lessons loves teaches us is that not all love is healthy. Some love is laced with insecurity, control, or inconsistency. And when we've been hurt, we start to question our worth, our trust, even our capacity to love again. But hear this: someone else's inability to love you properly is not a reflection of your value. You are not too much. You are not too sensitive. You are not unlovable.

Healing begins when you stop chasing the love that hurt you, and start returning to yourself. The version of you that once smiled freely, that believed in magic, that gave without fear. You may not be that person right now but you can find your way back, piece by piece. Start small. Choose peace over closure. Choose solitude over temporary company. Choose your own heart, over and over, until it feels full again.

Love isn't just something you receive; it's something you can rebuild within. Through your boundaries. Through your kindness to yourself. Through your refusal to settle for less than what you deserve.

And when you're ready truly ready you'll find that love didn't leave you behind. It waited, patiently, for you to remember:

You are still worthy.

You are still enough.

And love, the kind that nurtures instead of wounds, will find you when you no longer need it to complete you but simply to walk beside you.

You loved deeply,

Maybe too deeply,

Believing in forever

Even when their hands felt temporary.

And now, here you are

Not broken,

But bent in places

No one else can see.

Let it be known:

Grief is not weakness.

Missing them does not make you foolish.

Still loving them does not make you stuck.

You are simply human,

With a heart brave enough to feel,

And soft enough to still hope.

But now,

It's time to return.

Return to your own breath,

To the sound of your laughter,

To the comfort of your silence.

Choose peace, even if it feels lonely.

Choose healing, even if it means letting go.

Choose yourself, even if you once believed

You weren't enough.

Because real love,

The kind that stays,

The kind that sees you,

The kind that doesn't ask you to shrink,

Is still out there.

But first,

Let it rise in you.

In your words,

In your patience.

In the way you learn to hold your own hand

When no one else does.

This isn't the end of your story.

It's the soft beginning.

Of a love that will never abandon you again.

Because this time,

It starts with you.

You are whole, even when no one else is near."

There's a quiet that comes after love.

At first, it feels like silence.

Then, it feels like emptiness.

And sometimes, it feels like pain.

Letting go is not forgetting,

It's not a blade, it's not a war,

It's standing in the empty space

And not reaching anymore.

It's learning how to breathe again

Without your name beneath each sigh,

It's choosing peace, despite the pull

To chase a love that said goodbye.

So I untie the threads between us,

Not in anger, but in grace,

Because holding on too tightly

Only leaves the soul misplaced.

I loved you more than words can show,

But even love must learn to go.

And in this quiet, aching end,

I lose a love...

To find myself again.

I built a home inside my chest

Where only you were meant to be,

But love is cruel when it's one-sided,

You packed your bags and set me free.

You didn't fight, you didn't flinch,

Just walked away like I was air,

And I was left to grieve a ghost

Of someone still alive somewhere.

I scream in silence every night,

Where your memory crawls back in

Not loud enough to bring you back,

But just enough to break me thin.

Letting go? It's not brave. It's brutal.

It's a war I wage alone.

It's choosing pain that's real and sharp

Over waiting for a love that's gone.

Still I'm learning how to breathe again

In a world you used to fill.

And though you never said goodbye...

I'm saying it now.

And meaning it.

Still.

I didn't know it was the last time,

The last laugh, the last touch, the last glance.

If I had known,

I would've memorized the sound of your voice,

Tattooed your goodbye into my skin.

You didn't say it was over.

You just... stopped showing up.

And I stayed,

With my hands open and my heart on the floor,

Begging for a reason that never came.

Letting go isn't peaceful.

It's violent in the quietest ways

It tears through the soul like a whisper,

Soft enough to miss,

Loud enough to ruin you.

But today, I choose to stop waiting.

Not because I'm healed

But because I deserve to live

Without breaking every time, I remember

That you chose not to stay.

You took the best parts of me

When you walked away.

Not because you stole them,

But because I gave them willingly.

I gave you my softness,

My laughter,

My unguarded heart.

And you handed back silence.

I replayed every moment,

Looking for the one

Where I stopped being enough.

But maybe I never was.

Letting go feels like failure.

Like losing a war I never asked to fight.

But I'm learning,

Sometimes surviving love

Is braver than staying in it.

So, this is not a goodbye.

It's a release.

Of you.

Of the girl I became trying to be loved.

Of the pain that taught me what I deserve.

You were the kind of love

That filled every room I walked into,

Until one day,

You weren't.

And now I hear my own footsteps echo

In places we once called ours,

And I wonder how silence

Can feel so loud.

I still dream of you sometimes,

Not in romance,

But in ache.

The kind that wakes me up

With a name I no longer say aloud.

Letting go is not a door I closed.

It's a window I stare out of every day,

Knowing you're somewhere

Living, laughing, forgetting.

While I am here,

Trying to remember

How it felt

To not miss someone

Who doesn't miss me.

You loved me

Like someone passing through,

Just enough to stay a while,

Not enough to stay for good.

I learned to read between your silences,

To shrink myself to fit your needs,

Thinking if I became softer,

You might finally hold me with both hands.

But you only ever reached for me

When it was convenient.

And I was too in love to notice

You never really stayed.

Letting go is not forgetting.

It's living with the knowing,

That I was almost,

Barely,

Half-loved.

And still, I gave you all of me.

Some loves don't end with a goodbye they just drift. One day you stop talking as often, the calls fade, the warmth softens. And yet, weeks or years later, they still visit your mind like a breeze through an open window. You'll be standing in line for coffee or watching the rain, and suddenly, there they are in the quiet, in the way you still remember their favourite joke or how they took their tea. It's not pain exactly it's something softer now, a familiar ache, like a scar that doesn't hurt but never quite disappears.

We don't always stop loving someone when they leave. Sometimes, we just learn to carry them differently. Not in our arms, but in our minds, like folded letters we never send. Love changes shape it becomes a lesson, a poem tucked behind ribs, a shadow that walks beside us when we feel most alone. And slowly, we realize it wasn't meant to stay forever. It was meant to show us what we deserve, what we need, and how deep we're capable of feeling. Some loves don't return but they leave us more human.

"Some people don't stay, but their love teaches you how deep your heart can go and how gently you must carry yourself after."

Some loves don't end, they slowly fade,

Like sunlight slipping into shade.

No final word, no crashing sound,

Just silence growing all around.

You find them in forgotten things,

In songs, in smells, in silver rings.

A laugh you hear across the street,

The ghost of them in strangers' feet.

You learn to live with what remains,

The warmth, the weight, the quiet pains.

Not holding tight, not letting go.

Just walking with the undertow.

They taught you love, they showed you
ache,

They cracked you open, made you break.

But in the breaking, something grew.

A softer heart, a deeper you.

I gave my heart without a sound,

Hoping you'd catch its fall.

But you were blind to all I gave

Unmoved beyond my call.

I wore the weight of silent tears,

Of dreams that never grew.

Yet in the silence of your absence,

I slowly found what's true.

For love unreturned still shapes us whole,

Still teaches how to feel,

And from the ruins of what was,

I built a love that heals.

"Even the love that wasn't returned still taught me how deeply I could feel—and how fully I deserve to be loved in return."

It's okay to miss them,

Even as you walk away.

Grief is not weakness,

It's proof you cared all the way.

You don't have to forget the moments,

You don't have to erase the song.

But you can stop replaying

A place where you don't belong.

Letting go is not quitting.

It's choosing peace over pain.

It's whispering, "I loved you,"

And not needing to say it again.

You can let go now.

Not because they were small,

But because your heart is vast

And it's time to give it back to you.

"You did not lose love you returned it to its
source yourself."

You've done the hardest part,

You let go.

Even with shaking hands

And a heart that didn't want to.

You stood in the silence

And chose yourself,

Even when the memory of them

Pulled like gravity.

Now comes the light.

Not all at once,

But in small, steady ways

In mornings that don't ache,

In laughter that's truly yours,

In peace that finally stays.

You've felt the ache.

You've stood in the storm of memory,

Holding onto a love that slowly slipped away.

But this part of your story isn't about them anymore.

It's about you.

Your strength. Your softness. Your survival.

Letting go does not mean you didn't love them enough.

It means you finally loved yourself enough.

Enough to stop chasing silence.

Enough to choose peace over pain.

This next part?

It belongs to your healing.

To rediscovering joy in your own reflection.

To smiling again, without apology.

To knowing that the love you were willing to
give them,

You can now pour back into you.

"One day, your heart will thank you, not for
holding on, but for having the courage to
set itself free."

Dear You,

If no one has told you lately

You are worthy of a love that stays. A love that doesn't confuse you, silence you, or make you feel like you have to earn it every day. You are not too much, too quiet, too complicated, too broken. You are exactly enough. Just as you are.

I hope you stop settling for almost. For the kind of love that makes you question your value, your beauty, your heart. I hope you realize that the right love won't make you chase or shrink. It will feel like home, not a test.

And until that love comes, if it hasn't yet I hope you hold yourself the way you wished they held you. Speak to yourself gently. Show up for your heart. You deserve love that lifts you, and it starts with how you treat yourself. You were never meant to beg for love. You were meant to bloom in it.

So please, don't dim your light waiting for someone to notice. Burn bright. Someone out there is looking for that exact glow.

With love,

From someone who sees your worth.

Sometimes, you just love.

Silently.

Completely.

And let them go

Without them ever realizing what they
meant to you.

If any part of this book felt like home to your heart, please don't stay silent.

I'd love to know your story, the soft parts, the aching ones, the pieces you've never said out loud.

Come talk to me.

Write to me.

Share your heart—@meheksays on Instagram

ABOUT THE AUTHOR

Mehek sometimes called Mahi is a debut poet and writer who pours her heart into every word. She believes every feeling, silent struggle, and quiet love deserves to be heard. Through this first book, Mehek invites readers to find comfort and connection by sharing their own stories.

When she's not writing, she's dreaming, listening, and weaving emotions into verse and prose. You can reach out to her and share your story on Instagram: @meheksays